AF432390

Mighty God - Everlasting Father - Prince of Peace - Wonderful Counselor -
He
Shall Be
Called

<u>**Welcome! Advent 2020--And He Shall Be Called**</u>

For to us a child is born, to us a son is given; and the government shall be upon his shoulder, and his name shall be called Wonderful Counselor, Mighty God, Everlasting Father, Prince of Peace. Of the increase of his government and of peace there will be no end, on the throne of David and over his kingdom, to establish it and to uphold it with justice and with righteousness from this time forth and forevermore. The zeal of the Lord of hosts will do this. Isaiah 9:6-7

Advent is a most wonderful time of the year. Yes, I know, most people think that Christmas is the most wonderful time -- but it's really the anticipation that makes Christmas so wonderful. And Advent is all about anticipation. So what are we anticipating? What are we hoping for? Is it really as simple as a train set under the tree? Or do all the toys we dream of point us to bigger needs and deeper desires. A dream of an ordered world where even the most dangerous of situations are dealt with by a hero swooping in to save the day -- conveniently before we have to clean up for dinner.

In real life we are waiting. Waiting for someone to come and rescue us from this world of dangers filled. Who are we waiting for? Jesus. The prophets before Jesus longed for his appearing and the prophets after his birth anticipated his coming again. But just who is this baby, now Lord, who is coming again?

Read those words from Isaiah that are printed at the top of the page over again. When you do, they will begin to come alive with music... "For unto us a child is born... unto us... a son is given". If you lean in and listen close, the choir and orchestra will resonate in your heart with one of the famous sections of Handel's "Messiah".

What's interesting to me is just how deep the need Handel had for his Messiah to come! He was impossibly burdened with debt (and in those days debtors went to prison!). He was blind and in such poor health that his right side had become paralyzed. He was done and tempted to give up. But the needed rescue provided the creative fire inside him to write and finish a musical piece that lifts our hearts in anticipation of a true Son who can take the throne and be the hero to save the day.

And what kind of Hero do we need? One who is a Wonderful Counselor, a Mighty God, Everlasting Father and the Prince of Peace.

<u>**Start Here!**</u>

Mark 1:17 Follow me, and
I will make you become fishers of men

What in the world does that mean? We hear it all the time, "Follow Jesus"… but how do I do it?? And what, exactly, is Jesus going to make me into??
This booklet is a compilation of resources to help springboard you into a myriad of conversations with your family, friends and neighbors as we all share the Gospel, make disciples, and equip ambassadors for the world. We hope this will equip you, daily and practically, in following Jesus and helping others follow Him. We've broken down this book into a weekly devotion, daily readings of Scripture, a weekly Bible study for groups, and notes to help you go deeper, if needed.

Here's the key: **_You can do this_**.

We're convinced that if you jump in, read on your own, and with others – and look for the plain meaning – God himself will join you on the journey and guide you.

So, what to do first?

Step 1 - Set a time, daily, to read Scripture and reflect. There are readings for just five days a week so you can catch up on the weekend. Take as short as 15 minutes or as long as an hour if you want to really dig in.

Step 2 –Gather a group of people and decide to work through this together. It could be one other person, your family, or a group from work or the neighborhood. Groups keep the Bible as the main curriculum, help focus us on the Gospel and Growth, have between 3-12 people, and help us apply the Bible to our lives and the lives of those around us. Nobody was designed to live the Christian life alone. Join a group of friends and grow forward together!

Step 3 – Share what you're learning! Keep it simple and share what you've learned (questions, struggles and celebrations). If you need help, we're here to coach!

How to lead a Life Group

Perhaps you've been leading Bible Studies for a long time… or maybe this is your first attempt. Either way, know that we're here to coach and guide you! Here are some simple things to keep in mind and a brief outline as you begin:

First, realize what a Life Group is. It's not a book club, lecture society, or sensitivity training. A Life Group's goal is to apply the Gospel to everyday life as we intersect with the Bible.

A Life Group Defined

1 – A weekly meeting where the Bible is the one curriculum
2 – Two targets: The Gospel and Discipleship Engines
3 – 12 People… once it gets larger discussion is hindered
4 – Questions to help apply to real life.

Purpose - Discipleship = Follow, Form, Fulfill

"Making Disciples" means we are helping people move into being followers of Jesus, to people who are being formed by Jesus, to people who are fulfilling the great commission. We are sharing the Gospel, making Disciples, and equipping Ambassadors.

Rules of the Road

#1 BE SELF-AWARE not AUDIENCE AWARE: Be self-aware of how you personally affect the group through your words, actions, and non-verbal communication. Use "I" statements about what you think/feel… and make sure everyone talks. No preaching! Let Jesus (through his Word) fix people. Give encouragement; speak truth, point to Jesus.
#2 CONFIDENTIALITY: What's said in the group stays in the group.
#3 LISTEN: (PAUSE and SILENCE and No "Cross Talk") Value one another during the discussions. Don't think about what to say next. Affirm what's being said right now. Take a breath and think about what's just been said before responding. And don't fill the silence… Stay in the moment… be considerate… listen.   No side conversations.

Open – Help the group focus on the reason they're there

Start by checking in. Ask what people learned the previous week and shared with anyone. This will help move people from "information" to "transformation".

"Open" questions help break the ice and get people relating with each other and the text.

A great opening question will tie real life with the theme of the text… and it helps get people on task in a fun relational manner.

Bible Passage - *Leader: Tell the story in your own words, asking the group to re-tell it back to you.*
This method is called "Storying" and it helps people to engage with the story. It doesn't replace the reading of God's Word, but it does help people focus and hear things they might not have from the text. After they've heard the passage, and re-told it to you, read the passage.

Dig - Ask the questions in the book OR create new questions with simple journalist investigation. The point of these questions is to dig into the who, what, where, when, why facts of the passage. This helps keep the Bible the main teacher. Everyone has an opinion, but we always want to go back to what the text says. Help everyone keep in mind that the Bible is God's Word, all of it, so we need to let it teach us… rather than simply being commentators.

Apply - This is where a group really learns to grow. In order to apply the Gospel to daily living, it's important to ask these four kinds of questions. They help us see God's character and actions and contrast them to people's (and our!) character and actions. Once we see that, the Good News begins to come into focus. And, if you can identify the Good News then it's easy to share it with others.
1. What did you learn about God? (His character, ways, concerns)
2. What did you learn about people? (yourself?)
3. What does God do for us? In what way does this point to what Jesus does for us that we can't do on our own? How is this passage Good News rather than Good Advice?
4. What do we (I) need to do? Who do I need to share this with?

Pray - *Thank you / Sorry / Please*
Invite everyone to pray together as a group. Keep it simple, inviting everyone to pray, out loud, with simplicity. Simply list the thing(s) you're thankful for in prayer. Then share what you're sorry for. (Perhaps something in this study reminded you of something about God you need to remember, or something you need to do that you've neglected.) Then, going around as a group, individually and list out your requests. (Ask God to please help you with what you need to do… or help you in another area).

<u>**Week 1 – Wonderful Counselor**</u>
Week 1 Day 1   Genesis 3:8-13

8 And they heard the sound of the Lord God walking in the garden in the cool of the day, and the man and his wife hid themselves from the presence of the Lord God among the trees of the garden.

9 But the Lord God called to the man and said to him, "Where are you?" 10 And he said, "I heard the sound of you in the garden, and I was afraid, because I was naked, and I hid myself." 11 He said, "Who told you that you were naked? Have you eaten of the tree of which I commanded you not to eat?"

12 The man said, "The woman whom you gave to be with me, she gave me fruit of the tree, and I ate." 13 Then the Lord God said to the woman, "What is this that you have done?" The woman said, "The serpent deceived me, and I ate."

<u>**Devotional**</u>
God is a wonderful counselor. Why? Because he asks great questions. One of the amazing things about life -- is that it comes with scars. Life, we assume, starts beautifully -- a miracle. But reality soon sets in. Scars and wounds come from the challenges of children lost, friendships hurt, villains triumphing and injustice all around. If we're not careful, we are tempted to blame God -- yet what we see in Genesis 3 is that the problem is us. We have this human propensity to foul things up (sin) and we're really good at it!

In the beginning of all creation, God created a beautiful couple and put them in an idyllic setting. Everything they needed was there. Physically, spiritually, emotionally; at every level of human existence their needs were met. They were truly free.

They had two wonderful jobs to do: name the animals and procreate. Not a bad job description. But, when an enemy of God came into the garden and tempted them with the one thing in all their world that was forbidden -- they bit. They rebelled against God and their consequence was the knowledge of good and evil. Oh, how I would love to go back to a time of ignorance of evil!

But their rebellion is met with something strange. No immediate angelic guards coming to take them away. No courtroom bailiffs ushering them in to explain themselves. Instead, God comes to them and takes a walk. On on this walk he asks three important questions. Where are you? Who told you of nakedness? What have you done?

These three important questions are diagnostic. God has not lost their GPS tracking signal -- no, the question of where they are is relational. Where are they in relationship to God? Who told you? Their nakedness had never been a problem -- in fact, it was a celebration of safety! Yet now they are covering up, shamed, afraid of being truly seen. God wants to know who is shaming them. And third, "What have you done?" It's a question that is most strange for one caught in the act of rebellion to answer. Everyone in the story, including the reader, knows fully the depth of their action and the consequence. But God wants to help them own their brokenness.

God asks wonderful questions so that his favorite people in the entire universe will come to see the reality of their desperate situations. Scars and wounds acknowledged -- now, the medicine of hope can be administered.

<u>Reflection Question:</u>
What is a question that the Counselor God may be asking of you?

Week 1 Day 2   Isaiah 40:1-11

*40: 1 Comfort, comfort my people, says your God. 2 Speak
tenderly to Jerusalem, and proclaim to her that her hard service
has been completed, that her sin has been paid for, that she has
received from the Lord's hand double for all her sins.*

*3 A voice of one calling: "In the wilderness prepare the way for the
Lord[a];make straight in the desert a highway for our God.[b]
4 Every valley shall be raised up, every mountain and hill made
low; the rough ground shall become level, the rugged places a
plain. 5 And the glory of the Lord will be revealed, and all people
will see it together. For the mouth of the Lord has spoken."*

*6 A voice says, "Cry out." And I said, "What shall I cry? "All people
are like grass, and all their faithfulness is like the flowers of the
field.   7 The grass withers and the flowers fall, because the breath
of the Lord blows on them. Surely the people are grass. 8 The
grass withers and the flowers fall, but the word of our God endures
forever."*

*9 You who bring good news to Zion, go up on a high mountain.
You who bring good news to Jerusalem,[c] lift up your voice with a
shout, lift it up, do not be afraid; say to the towns of Judah, "Here
is your God!" 10 See, the Sovereign Lord comes with power, and
he rules with a mighty arm, See, his reward is with him, and his
recompense accompanies him.*

*11 He tends his flock like a shepherd: He gathers the lambs in his
arms and carries them close to his heart, he gently leads those
that have young.*

<u>Devotional</u>

Isaiah, speaking centuries before Jesus, says these amazing
words, "Comfort, comfort my people, says your God. Speak
tenderly to Jerusalem, and cry to her that her warfare is ended,
that her iniquity is pardoned, that she has received from the Lord's
hand double for all her sins." He was speaking to his people, in
Babylon, to remind them that God is for them. But they're having

trouble understanding it. Like an abused victim of the world -- a "good life" seems like a fantasy that is hopelessly out of reach.

I'm reminded of a story by Gordon MacDonald who was visiting with an Alcoholics Anonymous group:

One morning Kathy—I guessed her age at 35—joined us for the first time. One look at her face caused me to conclude that she must have been Hollywood-beautiful at 21. Now her face was swollen, her eyes red, her teeth rotting. Her hair looked unwashed, uncombed for who knows how long. "I've been in five states in the past month," she said. "I've slept under bridges on several nights. Been arrested. Raped. Robbed (now weeping). I don't know what to do. I … don't … want … to … be … homeless … any more. But (sob) I can't stop drinking (sob). I can't stop (sob). I can't … "

Next to Kathy was a rather large woman, Marilyn, sober for more than a dozen years. She reached with both arms toward Kathy and pulled her close, so close that Kathy's face was pressed to Marilyn's ample breast. I was close enough to hear Marilyn speak quietly into Kathy's ear, "Honey, you're going to be OK. You're with us now. We can deal with this together. All you have to do is keep coming. Hear me? Keep on coming." And then Marilyn kissed the top of Kathy's head.

I was awestruck. The simple words, the affection, the tenderness. How Jesus-like.

If we will just admit it -- we are all like Kathy. We're living in a broken world caused by our own brokenness and the brokenness of all around us. But God steps in -- with words of comfort. God will repay us double comfort for the trouble we've been in. And like a wonderful counselor, he meets us where we are and helps us see a new reality right in front of us.

Reflection Question:
What word or words of comfort do you need to hear from the Wonderful Counselor God today?

Is there someone who needs to hear you speaking God's comfort to them this week?

Week 1 Day 3   Psalm 85: 8-9

8 Let me hear what God the Lord will speak, for he will speak peace to his people, to his saints; but let them not turn back to folly.

9 Surely his salvation is near to those who fear him, that glory may dwell in our land.

Devotional

One of the challenges of needing counsel is asking, "Who should I go to"? In times of old, people would go to aunts, uncles, or an elder of the community. But increasingly that is made difficult by how far apart we live -- leaving our hometowns for remote opportunities. Since 1950, the United States has increased professional caregivers a hundredfold. We have more than 450,000 psychologists, social workers, counselors, therapists and life coaches not to mention non-clinical social workers and substance abuse counselors.

In the book *Bad Religion*, Ross Douthat argues that as families have weakened and true friendships have waned, we have tried to fill the vacuum by relying on professional caregivers.
Douthat, quoting philosopher Ronald Dworkin says: "Most of these professionals spend their days helping people cope with everyday life problems," Dworkin writes, "not true mental illness." This means that "under our very noses a revolution has occurred in the personal dimension of life, such that millions of Americans must now pay professionals to listen to their everyday life problems." Douthat concludes: "The result is a nation where gurus and therapists have filled the roles once occupied by spouses and friends."

God promises something better. As our wonderful counselor, He is willing to speak to us -- and hear us! In Psalm 85:8 we hear the writer asking to "hear what God will speak". At the most, a counselor can diagnose problems and help us come up with a self-directed path forward. If we're in a hole, a mental health professional can confirm that we're in the hole and suggest various ways to get out -- on our own.

But the Psalmist is not in a hole -- he is hanging off the side of a cliff and doesn't have the strength to get back up on his own. He needs someone to solve the problem for him. And that's where his faith is found. He trusts that the Wonderful Counselor will speak. Think about that for a minute. Even though he is in trouble the writer is confident that God won't abandon him.

The God of the Universe cares so much about his people not just as a whole but individually that we can have confidence that he will speak. But what He speaks is better than we deserve. Our Wonderful Counselor comes not only with diagnosis and comfort that there is a way out but with "peace" that won't let us "turn back to folly". Our God doesn't leave us hanging -- but brings salvation near.

Reflection Question:
What are some of the ways that God speaks to people today? Have you ever heard Him speak to you? Take time to be still and listen for His wonderful counseling voice today.

Week 1 Day 4   2 Peter 3:8-18

8 But do not overlook this one fact, beloved, that with the Lord one day is as a thousand years, and a thousand years as one day. 9 The Lord is not slow to fulfill his promise as some count slowness, but is patient toward you, not wishing that any should perish, but that all should reach repentance. 10 But the day of the Lord will come like a thief, and then the heavens will pass away with a roar, and the heavenly bodies will be burned up and dissolved, and the earth and the works that are done on it will be exposed.

11 Since all these things are thus to be dissolved, what sort of people ought you to be in lives of holiness and godliness, 12 waiting for and hastening the coming of the day of God, because of which the heavens will be set on fire and dissolved, and the heavenly bodies will melt as they burn! 13 But according to his promise we are waiting for new heavens and a new earth in which righteousness dwells.

14 Therefore, beloved, since you are waiting for these, be diligent to be found by him without spot or blemish, and at peace. 15 And count the patience of our Lord as salvation, just as our beloved brother Paul also wrote to you according to the wisdom given him, 16 as he does in all his letters when he speaks in them of these matters. There are some things in them that are hard to understand, which the ignorant and unstable twist to their own destruction, as they do the other Scriptures.

17 You therefore, beloved, knowing this beforehand, take care that you are not carried away with the error of lawless people and lose your own stability. 18 But grow in the grace and knowledge of our Lord and Savior Jesus Christ. To him be the glory both now and to the day of eternity. Amen.

Devotional

A Wonderful Counselor? I feel like that title could only be reserved for someone who knew all my flaws and wasn't shocked -- but patient, knowing that in due course, the anger, frustration and devastation of failure would be fully known. But in being known the blessing of being understood and loved would begin to dawn.

R. O. Blechman is one of the most famous illustrators in the world. In his recent book, *Dear James: Letters to a Young Illustrator*, he shares a series of letters that he wrote to a younger fellow-illustrator. In one of the most poignant letters, Blechman addresses the reality of failure:

> *"Preliminary drawings and sketches often are discouraging things, pale shadows of one's bold intentions. Seemingly nonsense, they're especially dispiriting for beginners ... 'Is that what I did,' the novice might ask, 'and I consider myself an artist?! ... Speaking for myself (but also for other illustrators, I'm sure), my trash basket is full of false starts and failed drawings ... There should be a Museum of Failed Art. It would exhibit all the terrible art that would have ended up in trash bins and garbage cans, lost and unknown to the public life."*

A Museum of Failed Disciples already exists. Just look at the Bible: Abraham, Moses, David, Solomon, Peter, Paul each one a complete failure in their own spectacular way. Yet, God is so very patient! Peter says, in 2 Peter 3:17... "take care that you are not carried away with the error of lawless people and lose your own stability. But grow in the grace and knowledge of our Lord and Savior Jesus Christ.

Jesus, as our Wonderful Counselor, listens patiently to our myriad failures and gently guides us to a knowing grace that accepts us where we are and loves us, in spite of us.

<u>Reflection Question:</u>
Do you have a failure that haunts you? Take some time to share that with Jesus. Let Him listen to you. Let him be your Wonderful Counselor.

Week 1 Day 5 Mark 1:1-18

1 The beginning of the gospel of Jesus Christ, the Son of God.

2 As it is written in Isaiah the prophet, "Behold, I send my messenger before your face, who will prepare your way, 3 the voice of one crying in the wilderness: 'Prepare the way of the Lord, make his paths straight,'"

4 John appeared, baptizing in the wilderness and proclaiming a baptism of repentance for the forgiveness of sins. 5 And all the country of Judea and all Jerusalem were going out to him and were being baptized by him in the river Jordan, confessing their sins. 6 Now John was clothed with camel's hair and wore a leather belt around his waist and ate locusts and wild honey. 7 And he preached, saying, "After me comes he who is mightier than I, the strap of whose sandals I am not worthy to stoop down and untie. 8 I have baptized you with water, but he will baptize you with the Holy Spirit."

9 In those days Jesus came from Nazareth of Galilee and was baptized by John in the Jordan. 10 And when he came up out of the water, immediately he saw the heavens being torn open and the Spirit descending on him like a dove. 11 And a voice came from heaven, "You are my beloved Son; with you I am well pleased."

12 The Spirit immediately drove him out into the wilderness. 13 And he was in the wilderness forty days, being tempted by Satan. And he was with the wild animals, and the angels were ministering to him.

14 Now after John was arrested, Jesus came into Galilee, proclaiming the gospel of God, 15 and saying, "The time is fulfilled, and the kingdom of God is at hand; repent and believe in the gospel."16 Passing alongside the Sea of Galilee, he saw Simon and Andrew the brother of Simon casting a net into the sea, for they were fishermen. 17 And Jesus said to them, "Follow me, and I will make you become fishers of men." 18 And immediately they left their nets and followed him.

<u>**Devotional**</u>

When John comes onto the scene, in Mark 1, his charge is to make straight paths for the Messiah. What does that look like? If we keep reading, it is clear that "repentance for the forgiveness of sins" is the straight path.

But a straight path to where? To our Wonderful Counselor. In the beginning, right after the Fall of Humanity in the first sin, God comes and asks questions. The purpose of those questions was to make straight paths. But what's interesting is the weird images that are intersecting. We're making straight paths for God to come to us -- not for us to go to God. But if we're making a path for God to come to us -- and it's not a path we're meant to travel -- then what's the nature of the path?

Think with me for a minute. What does our path in life normally look like? If we were to map it out, even the best planners among us would have a path that looked (at best) like a ball of twine that was unraveled across a map. We think we're headed one direction, two steps forward, one step back -- three steps right and two steps left -- and so on throughout life. The Israelites took a journey like that in the Old Testament -- it was a 40 year wilderness wandering on a trip that should (at most) take 4 weeks, walking. Round and round we go... where we end, we sure don't know.

But God does. Preparing a straight path for God simply means sitting down. We simply need to stop the twirling, panicked, back and forth careening down the road of life, and wait for God to come to us.

Jesus is the Wonderful Counselor. But unlike any other counselor that we have to set appointments for and drive to -- He will come to us if we just ask.

<u>**Reflection Question:**</u>
Do you have a time in your life when the "straight path" (your plans for your life) was derailed and the wilderness or alternate path became the plan from God for you? How do you see God as a Wonderful Counselor in those circumstances in your life?

Week 1 Bible Study -Isaiah 40:1-11 – Wonderful Counselor

Open
- How did you see the truth of God's Word in your life this past week? Where did you see Jesus at work this week?
- What was the most exciting news you ever received? Why was it so welcome?

Dig *(Read the passage: Isaiah 40:1-11)*
1. What questions, concerns, new things did you discover?
2. In 587 BC Jerusalem is sacked and its people deported by Babylon, the new world power. Given this situation, what does Isaiah's emphatic "comfort" mean to Israel?
3. What images does the Lord use to assure His people of His forgiveness?
4. In Isaiah's time the coming of a king was announced by a herald. People literally leveled the roads the king would travel. What king is in view in verses 3-5?
5. What does it mean to prepare the way for Him?
6. The Gospels quote verse 3 in reference to John the Baptist preparing the way of Jesus. What does that imply about the identity of Jesus?
7. How can you "prepare the way" in your life for Jesus? What needs leveling or shoring up?
8. Jesus comes as Shepherd (v.11) as well as King. How do you see him as a Wonderful Counselor in his shepherding of you?

Apply
1. What did you learn about God? (His character, ways, concerns)
2. What did you learn about people? (yourself?)
3. What does God do for us? In what way does this point to what Jesus does for us that we can't do on our own? How is this passage Good News rather than Good Advice?
4. What do we (I) need to do?
5. Who do I need to share this with?

Pray - Thank you / Sorry / Please

<u>**Week 2 – Mighty God**</u>
<u>Week 2 Day 1</u>   Isaiah 65:17-25

17 "For behold, I create new heavens and a new earth, and the former things shall not be remembered or come into mind. 18 But be glad and rejoice forever in that which I create; for behold, I create Jerusalem to be a joy, and her people to be a gladness. 19 I will rejoice in Jerusalem and be glad in my people; no more shall be heard in it the sound of weeping and the cry of distress. 20 No more shall there be in it an infant who lives but a few days, or an old man who does not fill out his days, for the young man shall die a hundred years old, and the sinner a hundred years old shall be accursed.

21 They shall build houses and inhabit them; they shall plant vineyards and eat their fruit. 22 They shall not build and another inhabit; they shall not plant and another eat; for like the days of a tree shall the days of my people be, and my chosen shall long enjoy the work of their hands. 23 They shall not labor in vain or bear children for calamity, for they shall be the offspring of the blessed of the Lord, and their descendants with them.

24 Before they call I will answer; while they are yet speaking I will hear. 25 The wolf and the lamb shall graze together; the lion shall eat straw like the ox, and dust shall be the serpent's food. They shall not hurt or destroy in all my holy mountain," says the Lord.

<u>**Devotional**</u>
In the Chronicles of Narnia, C.S. Lewis describes a world that is controlled by a witch who has made it "always winter and never Christmas".

In one amazing scene, four children are talking to Mr. and Mrs. Beaver (which is exactly as fanciful as you might imagine). In the midst of their discussions, they hear a sleigh coming along the path they're traveling, and they scurry off to hide -- surely it's the witch. But then they see someone very different.

It was a sled, and it was reindeer with bells on their harness. But they were far bigger than the Witch's reindeer, and they were not white but brown. And on the sled sat a person whom everyone knew the moment they set eyes on him. He was a huge man in a bright red robe (bright as holly berries) with a hood that had fur inside it and a great white beard that fell like a foamy waterfall over his chest. Everyone knew him because, though you see people of this sort only in Narnia, you see pictures of them and hear them talked about even in our world – the world on this side of the wardrobe door. But when you really see them in Narnia it is rather different. Some of the pictures of Father Christmas in our world make him look only funny and jolly. But now that the children actually stood looking at him they didn't find it quite like that. He was so big, and so glad, and so real, that they all became quite still. They felt very glad, but also solemn. "I've come at last," said he. "She has kept me out for a long time, but I have got in al last. Aslan is on the move. The Witch's magic is weakening."

The story is a great reminder that God is moving -- something which Isaiah's imagination picks up on and explains in a series of "never agains" and "but now" statements. Cry and distress are replaced with Rejoicing. Premature death is replaced with long life. Building for others without reward is replaced with enjoying the work of your hands. Like a tree after a frost, there is pent up energy ready to explode in a riot of buds and fruit.

Sometimes the harsh frosts of this life—cancer, divorce, bankruptcy, trauma, grief, depression—cause our hearts to freeze. It seems like it's always winter… and never Christmas… BUT, take heart… Aslan IS on the move… God will use His might to set things right.

<u>Reflection Question:</u>
What signs do you see in your life that a Mighty God is on the move in your circumstances?

Week 2 Day 2 Psalm 126

126:1 When the Lord restored the fortunes of Zion,
* we were like those who dream.*
2 Then our mouth was filled with laughter,
* and our tongue with shouts of joy;*
then they said among the nations,
* "The Lord has done great things for them."*
3 The Lord has done great things for us;
* we are glad.*

4 Restore our fortunes, O Lord,
* like streams in the Negeb!*
5 Those who sow in tears
* shall reap with shouts of joy!*
6 He who goes out weeping,
* bearing the seed for sowing,*
shall come home with shouts of joy,
* bringing his sheaves with him.*

Devotional

In Psalm 126 there is a twin reality: 1. The Lord has done great things, and, 2. God, restore our fortunes. The reality the Psalmist faces is that God has a very long track record of acting on behalf of His people -- but sometimes, it seems like He is silent and not working at all.

One person who lived this dual reality was Dietrich Bonhoeffer. He was a true follower of Jesus who stood up to the Nazi regime rallying many Christians to oppose the horrors of Hitler. For his trouble, he was imprisoned and sentenced to death.

While in prison he wrote that
> *"Everything has its time, and the main thing is that we keep step with God, and do not keep pressing on a few steps ahead -- nor keep dawdling a step behind. It's presumptuous to want to have everything at once --*

*matrimonial bliss, the cross, and the heavenly
Jerusalem, where they neither marry or are given in
marriage. Everything has its time."*

Indeed, everything has its time -- and the complete fulfillment of
God's plan takes time. But that doesn't mean he is not acting --
just that we are learning to wait. Simply waiting on Him shows our
dependence upon Him as our Mighty God, for in waiting, we
choose Him over all other possible saviors. As Eugene Peterson
once said, "Waiting doesn't diminish us any more than it
diminishes a pregnant mother".

Dietrich Bonhoeffer lived that dual reality of God's past work and
seeming silence. While he never was able to get married to his
fiancé, years later she released this gem from his letters to her:

> *" A prison cell, [where] one waits, hopes, does various
> unessential things, and is completely dependent on the
> fact that the door of freedom has to be opened from the
> outside is not a bad picture of Advent."*

Dietrich was killed a few months later, in the spring. Advent never
seemed to give way to celebration on Earth. In fact, he was put to
death just shy of 30 days before the end of the war. But in that
cell, Dietrich realized salvation as he rose into the arms of his
Mighty God.

<u>Reflection Question:</u>
What are you waiting for in your life? Where would you like a
Mighty God to act? What might He be teaching you in this waiting
time?

Week 2 Day 3   1 Thessalonians 5:12-28

12 We ask you, brothers, to respect those who labor among you and are over you in the Lord and admonish you, 13 and to esteem them very highly in love because of their work. Be at peace among yourselves. 14 And we urge you, brothers, admonish the idle, encourage the fainthearted, help the weak, be patient with them all. 15 See that no one repays anyone evil for evil, but always seek to do good to one another and to everyone. 16 Rejoice always, 17 pray without ceasing, 18 give thanks in all circumstances; for this is the will of God in Christ Jesus for you. 19 Do not quench the Spirit. 20 Do not despise prophecies, 21 but test everything; hold fast what is good. 22 Abstain from every form of evil.

23 Now may the God of peace himself sanctify you completely, and may your whole spirit and soul and body be kept blameless at the coming of our Lord Jesus Christ. 24 He who calls you is faithful; he will surely do it. 25 Brothers, pray for us. 26 Greet all the brothers with a holy kiss. 27 I put you under oath before the Lord to have this letter read to all the brothers.

28 The grace of our Lord Jesus Christ be with you.

Devotional

The old saying goes, "Power corrupts and absolute power corrupts absolutely".

An excellent display of this was made in 2012 when the owner of the New England Patriots football team told 60 Minutes that President Putin, of Russia, took his third Super Bowl Ring.

According to Kraft, who was at the Kremlin on a business trip, Putin was meeting the delegation and saw the ring. They talked, briefly, and Kraft took the ring off and showed all the various facets of the ring. Then, so that Putin could get a better look, Kraft handed him the ring. Putin put the king on his finger and then said, "I could kill someone with this ring" -- ostensibly because it is so massive. Then, according to Kraft, Putin put the ring in his pocket, three KGB agents surrounded Putin, and he walked out -- with Kraft's ring.

Absolute power corrupts in absolutely every instance except one. Jesus, the creator of the universe. He has legions of angels and other powerful beings to do his bidding, yet He labors with one purpose -- our salvation. And in so doing, his full and only expectation is gratitude.

Paul reminds the Thessalonians how Christians are called to live as both leaders and followers. Ultimately all as followers of Christ who are to live in peace with each other, serve each other patiently and show love to all. This is in direct contrast to worldly power—especially when we are told not to repay evil for evil, but seek to do good to each other. Finally, we are encouraged to give thanks in every circumstance. Seemingly simple, this command divests us of power as we see that all we have comes from God and we can simply thank Him for it.

God uses his mighty power to provide salvation and aid to his people in exchange for gratitude and peace. Absolute power, truly absolute power, brings peace and grace.

<u>Reflection Question:</u>
Which of these commands is hard for you to follow? Which is easy? What are you grateful to a Mighty God for today?

Week 2 Day 4   John 3:22-30

22 After this Jesus and his disciples went into the Judean countryside, and he remained there with them and was baptizing. 23 John also was baptizing at Aenon near Salim, because water was plentiful there, and people were coming and being baptized 24 (for John had not yet been put in prison).

25 Now a discussion arose between some of John's disciples and a Jew over purification. 26 And they came to John and said to him, "Rabbi, he who was with you across the Jordan, to whom you bore witness—look, he is baptizing, and all are going to him." 27 John answered, "A person cannot receive even one thing unless it is given him from heaven. 28 You yourselves bear me witness, that I said, 'I am not the Christ, but I have been sent before him.' 29 The one who has the bride is the bridegroom. The friend of the bridegroom, who stands and hears him, rejoices greatly at the bridegroom's voice. Therefore this joy of mine is now complete. 30 He must increase, but I must decrease."

Devotional

He is the mighty God. As he has wisdom, so he has strength, to go through with his undertaking; he is able to save to the utmost; and such is the work of the Mediator, that no less a power than that of the mighty God could accomplish it.—Matthew Henry

By all accounts, John the Baptizer was an impressive man. He convinced simple country folk and metropolitan sophisticates to come out to the middle of the desert wilderness not only to hear him -- but to be baptized. To shed all their pride, privacy and admit that they were in need of deep soul refreshing cleansing from their sins. Publicly.

But in the middle of this God directed revival of the nation -- the largest revival seen in over 500 years -- comes Jesus who essentially takes over. Rather than develop his own audience, Jesus comes in to steal John's. But John's reaction is on point.

John understands just who Jesus is. And in the middle of Jesus presenting himself to be baptized and identify with sinners -- God says something he hasn't said of anyone else. Here, with no mystery at all, Jesus is declared the son of God. Jesus is the Mighty God in a way no other could claim -- the Son of God.

Abraham was a friend of God.
Moses was the servant of God.
Aaron was the chosen of God.
David was the man after God's own heart.
Paul was the apostle of God.

But this unique title was reserved by God from the beginning through the prophets for the unique God-man Jesus.

And John the Baptizer's response was perfect. "I am not the Christ. He must increase, I must decrease"

In Advent we remind ourselves of just who we are. We are not God -- which is a great reminder for those of us concerned about power. And we are blessed most fully when we get off our high horse and let Jesus ride all the way to the throne as the God who is mightier than we are.

Reflection Question:
Which of the titles that are listed of people of God (friend of God, servant of God, chosen of God....) would you like to be true about you? How can a Mighty God help you become that type of person?

Week 2 Day 5   Revelation 7:9-12

9 After this I looked, and behold, a great multitude that no one could number, from every nation, from all tribes and peoples and languages, standing before the throne and before the Lamb, clothed in white robes, with palm branches in their hands, 10 and crying out with a loud voice, "Salvation belongs to our God who sits on the throne, and to the Lamb!"

11 And all the angels were standing around the throne and around the elders and the four living creatures, and they fell on their faces before the throne and worshiped God, 12 saying, "Amen! Blessing and glory and wisdom and thanksgiving and honor and power and might be to our God forever and ever! Amen."

Devotional

In J. R. R. Tolkien's book "The Return of the King" the kingdom is almost lost by a mighty and evil horde of orcs. An incredible battle ensues and the evil orc empire is defeated.

The final climactic scene illustrates what we can only imagine the rightful seating of Jesus as the Mighty God -- King of our Salvation -- might look like. Aragorn, the rightful king of the west, has labored in obscurity, gone without comforts normally afforded a king, served his subjects and battle for their lives. Finally, having prevailed over the forces of the dark lord's orc armies, he is poised to inter the city.

When Aragorn enters the fortified city of Mina Tirith for the first time as king, the city's steward proclaims Aragorn's royal pedigree for all the citizens to hear:

> *"Here is Aragorn son of Arathorn, chieftain of the Dunedain of Arnor, Captain of the Host of the West, bearer of the Star of the North, wielder of the Sword Reforged, victorious in battle, whose hands bring healing, the Elfstone, Elessar of the line of Valandil, Isildur's son, Elendil's son of Numenor. Shall he be king and enter into the City and dwell there?"*

Pastor Ken Langley, reflecting on this Mighty God and King draws the parallel to Jesus,

> *"There was another King who long labored in obscurity: unheralded, humbly serving the people over whom he had every right to reign, laying down his life for them. Today he claims the throne of our lives. Here is Jesus the Christ, the Second Adam, the Bright and Morning Star, the First and the Last, victorious in battle, whose hands bring healing, Mighty Second Person of the Trinity, Son of David, Son of Man, Word of God Incarnate, the Wonderful Counselor, the Mighty God, the Everlasting Father, the Prince of Peace. Shall he enter our hearts—our church—and dwell there?"*

<u>Reflection Question:</u>
Which name of Jesus resonates in your heart this Advent season? Why? What does it mean to you?

Week 2 Bible Study - Isaiah 65:17-25 – Mighty God

Open
- How did you see the truth of God's Word in your life this past week? Where did you see Jesus at work this week?
- As a child, how did you picture what heaven was like?

Dig *(Read the passage: Isaiah 65:17-25)*
1. What questions, concerns, new things did you discover?
2. What accounts for this new state of affairs for the Israelites?
3. What will life be like when the exiles are freed?
4. What promises are delivered in this section?
5. Which promise sounds the best to you?
6. How does the account of the creation and fall (Genesis 1-3) figure as the background to this passage?
7. What do we learn here about God's purposes and plans?
8. How does this new creation come into being for us? (see 2 Cor. 5:17)
9. Try to picture your life without any of the causes or results of grief, sin and pain. What would that free you to do?
10. How might this vision of what God will bring about affect the way you deal with the struggles you face right now?

Apply
1. What did you learn about God? (His character, ways, concerns)
2. What did you learn about people? (yourself?)
3. What does God do for us? In what way does this point to what Jesus does for us that we can't do on our own? How is this passage Good News rather than Good Advice?
4. What do we (I) need to do?
5. Who do I need to share this with?

Pray - Thank you / Sorry / Please

*4 From of old no one has heard or perceived by the ear,
no eye has seen a God besides you, who acts for those who wait
for him. 5 You meet him who joyfully works righteousness, those
who remember you in your ways. Behold, you were angry, and we
sinned; in our sins we have been a long time, and shall we be
saved?*

*6 We have all become like one who is unclean, and all our
righteous deeds are like a polluted garment. We all fade like a leaf,
and our iniquities, like the wind, take us away. 7 There is no one
who calls upon your name, who rouses himself to take hold of you;
for you have hidden your face from us, and have made us melt
in the hand of our iniquities.*

*8 But now, O Lord, you are our Father; we are the clay, and you
are our potter; we are all the work of your hand. 9 Be not so
terribly angry, O Lord, and remember not iniquity forever.
    Behold, please look, we are all your people.*

Devotional

The two people swept the child up and ran for the car. Driving at
over 90 miles per hour they held him tight so he couldn't get away.
There was no escape. There was nothing for him to do but cry --
and then it go worse. They arrived at a strange place with bright
lights, what looked like masked bandits, cruelly seized his limbs
and head so it was impossible to move. Then they injected
something so near his eye he could see the sharp point of the
needle. And then the pain and tugging as they went into his flesh.

It sounds like a horror story, doesn't it! And it probably was
horrifying from my son Caleb's perspective! And what made it

worse was that his own Father seemed to be at the center of all his pain. But reality was quite different.

You see, at 2 years old, Caleb was just the right height to bump into coffee tables and need stitches. Yes, his Father had broken the speed limit in our Honda mini-van. And yes, we did hold him down so he couldn't move. And yes, needles were involved.

But, the reason for all of that was so that he could be healed. The bone sticking out of the wound needed to have flesh sewn over it. The pain had a purpose. All he needed to do -- all he could do was wait.

In the same way, humanity has been inflicted with a horrible wound and God must step in and bring healing. But from our vantage point it's hard to tell what God is doing sometimes. We are his people -- and He is our Father -- but the rending of the heavens seems so very dangerous! And the sufferings we sometimes have to endure seem so capricious. But the purpose is found in Jesus who teaches us to pray, "Our Father... deliver us from evil." In that deliverance Jesus takes on our pain and we wait for Him to heal us. And, He does.

<u>Reflection Question:</u>
Has there been a time in your life where you endured suffering that seemed purposeless? Can you see a purpose in it now looking back? If not yet, can you trust the Everlasting Father God who tells you of His love and shows it in His son, Jesus?

*80:1 Give ear, O Shepherd of Israel, you who lead Joseph like a flock. You who are enthroned upon the cherubim, shine forth.
2 Before Ephraim and Benjamin and Manasseh, stir up your might and come to save us!*

3 Restore us, O God; let your face shine, that we may be saved!

*14 Turn again, O God of hosts! Look down from heaven, and see; have regard for this vine, 15 the stock that your right hand planted, and for the son whom you made strong for yourself.
16 They have burned it with fire; they have cut it down; may they perish at the rebuke of your face!*

17 But let your hand be on the man of your right hand, the son of man whom you have made strong for yourself. 18 Then we shall not turn back from you; give us life, and we will call upon your name!

*19 Restore us, O Lord God of hosts!
Let your face shine, that we may be saved!*

Devotional

We long for God to restore us -- to bring us out of the darkness of our times of troubles and lift us up to freedom. Yet, we have a mistaken understanding of freedom. We believe freedom is the ability to do whatever we want. I think this is why there's this silly discussion of free will that Christians sometimes devolve into. But the reality is that all wills are bound to something and only when we're bound to the right thing we have life and true freedom.

Luther describes the state of the human heart as a "bound will". Or, as St. Paul would say, "What we want to do, we don't do -- and what we do, we don't want to do." As the Psalmist recognizes, our natural state is like a vine that is not protected -- without wall or barrier -- nothing to keep us from being plucked or ravaged. When the Psalm says, "restore us", it's asking for a wall to be established.

My kids are amazing musicians. They love to play their instruments and they're quite good. One of the necessary realities of their ability is that they are bound, for hours and hours, with no seeming freedom. We aren't that dramatic in our house (most of the time) -- we just call it "practice". Gabbi is our most prolific "practicer" and will play for hours in her room -- but the discipline of practice is the price of freedom.

You see, everyone is bound to something. But if the nature of what we are bound to is good, then the fruit is a freedom of being like what we're bound to.

Our Eternal Father is willing to curtail our freedom -- by building a wall around us. Our natural will says, "don't fence me in" -- but if we know the nature of the Father -- we realize that such a construct actually creates freedom to become who we were created to be.

Reflection Question:

Where are you asking the Everlasting Father God to restore you this Advent? Do you feel bound by something that is not pleasing to Him? Confess it, give it to God and ask Him to build a wall of protection around you.

Week 3 Day 3 1 Corinthians 1:1-9

1 Paul, called by the will of God to be an apostle of Christ Jesus, and our brother Sosthenes, 2 To the church of God that is in Corinth, to those sanctified in Christ Jesus, called to be saints together with all those who in every place call upon the name of our Lord Jesus Christ, both their Lord and ours:

3 Grace to you and peace from God our Father and the Lord Jesus Christ.

4 I give thanks to my God always for you because of the grace of God that was given you in Christ Jesus, 5 that in every way you were enriched in him in all speech and all knowledge— 6 even as the testimony about Christ was confirmed among you— 7 so that you are not lacking in any gift, as you wait for the revealing of our Lord Jesus Christ, 8 who will sustain you to the end, guiltless in the day of our Lord Jesus Christ. 9 God is faithful, by whom you were called into the fellowship of his Son, Jesus Christ our Lord.

Devotional

In, *Cure for the Common Life*, Max Lucado tells this wonderful story:

> *The bank sent me an overdraft notice on the checking account of one of my daughters. I encourage my college-age girls to monitor their accounts. Even so, they sometimes overspend.*

> *What should I do? Send her an angry letter? Admonition might help her later, but it won't satisfy the bank. Phone and tell her to make a deposit? Might as well tell a fish to fly. I know her liquidity. Zero. Transfer the money from my account to hers? Seemed to be the best option. After all, I had $25.37. I could replenish her account and pay the overdraft fee as well. Since she calls me Dad, I did what dads do. I covered my daughter's mistake.*

When I told her she was overdrawn, she said she was sorry. Still, she offered no deposit. She was broke. She had one option, "Dad, could you…" "Honey," I interrupted, "I already have." I met her need before she knew she had one.

Long before you knew you needed grace, your Father did the same. He made an ample deposit. Before you knew you needed a Savior, you had one. And when you ask him for mercy, he answers, "Dear child. I've already given it."

<u>Reflection Question:</u>

When have you seen God as Everlasting Father extend grace or mercy to you in your life?

Week 3 Day 4   Romans 8:12-17

12 So then, brothers, we are debtors, not to the flesh, to live according to the flesh. 13 For if you live according to the flesh you will die, but if by the Spirit you put to death the deeds of the body, you will live.

14 For all who are led by the Spirit of God are sons of God. 15 For you did not receive the spirit of slavery to fall back into fear, but you have received the Spirit of adoption as sons, by whom we cry, "Abba! Father!"

16 The Spirit himself bears witness with our spirit that we are children of God, 17 and if children, then heirs—heirs of God and fellow heirs with Christ, provided we suffer with him in order that we may also be glorified with him.

Devotional

This passage in Romans reminds us that we must depend on the Holy Spirit to father spiritual children. It is not a work that we do in our own strength, but only in His power. Pastor Francis Chan shared this story in the magazine *Leadership Journal*:

I cannot make someone fall in love with Jesus.

It really came home for me, literally, with my own teenage daughter, who, 18 months ago, was not in love with Jesus. I spent nights crying, bawling, praying to the Lord. Here I am known for my ability to communicate, but there was nothing I could do for my own daughter that would make her fall in love with Jesus. Of course I could still guide and lead her, but I was powerless to convict her.

I prayed, "God, either your Spirit comes into her or your Spirit doesn't. It doesn't matter how great a dad I am. I cannot bring her to life."

One day she came into my room and said, "You were right, Dad. The Holy Spirit was not in me. But now he is." She talked about how near she was to God and how everything had changed. My wife and I were skeptical. We wanted to see evidence of change. But 18 months later, I can say she really is a new creation. I didn't do that. It was the Holy Spirit.

The Holy Spirit empowers us to become children of God. This work is done by Jesus on the Cross. C.S. Lewis states: "The Son of God became man to enable men to become the sons of God."

We stand humbled and awed that the King of the Universe desires to have us as His children. This desire is so strong that He would sacrifice His son to bring us back to Him. We can only respond in whole-hearted wonder and thankfulness to Him. Jane Marchant, in A Window on Eternity sums it this way:

> To say to God "Our Father"
> Is wondering gratitude,
> Is ardent venturing awe,
> Is humble penitence,
> Is reverential praise,
> Is endless fellowship,
> Is all-committing love
> To say "our Father"
> Truly, is
> To pray.

Reflection Question:

Spend time meditating on the fact that you are an adopted child of God. If you feel this isn't true of you, ask a pastor or priest to tell you how to become one. It is the most important decision you will ever make! God desires to be your Everlasting Father.

24 "But in those days, after that tribulation, the sun will be darkened, and the moon will not give its light, 25 and the stars will be falling from heaven, and the powers in the heavens will be shaken. 26 And then they will see the Son of Man coming in clouds with great power and glory. 27 And then he will send out the angels and gather his elect from the four winds, from the ends of the earth to the ends of heaven.

28 "From the fig tree learn its lesson: as soon as its branch becomes tender and puts out its leaves, you know that summer is near. 29 So also, when you see these things taking place, you know that he is near, at the very gates. 30 Truly, I say to you, this generation will not pass away until all these things take place. 31 Heaven and earth will pass away, but my words will not pass away.

32 "But concerning that day or that hour, no one knows, not even the angels in heaven, nor the Son, but only the Father. 33 Be on guard, keep awake. For you do not know when the time will come. 34 It is like a man going on a journey, when he leaves home and puts his servants in charge, each with his work, and commands the doorkeeper to stay awake.

35 Therefore stay awake—for you do not know when the master of the house will come, in the evening, or at midnight, or when the rooster crows, or in the morning— 36 lest he come suddenly and find you asleep. 37 And what I say to you I say to all: Stay awake."

Devotional

In the fall of 1991, a car driven by a drunk driver jumped its lane and smashed headfirst into a minivan driven by Jerry Sittser. Sittser and three of his children survived, but Sittser's wife, four-year-old child, and mother died in the crash. Over the years Sittser has offered some profound reflections about loss, grief, and suffering. In his book *A Grace Revealed*, Sittser shares the following story about how his son David responded to the tragic accident.

My son David is—and always has been—quiet and reflective. After the accident, he was the least likely to talk about it; but when he chose to, he usually had something significant to say or ask. I had to be ready to respond to him when he sent cues indicating he was ready to talk. Our best conversations happened in the car. One particular conversation has stayed fresh in my memory. David was eight at the time; we were driving to a soccer match some distance from our home. Typical for these occasions, David was quiet. The car was full of silence—not a heavy silence, but a liquid silence, as if some question was brewing inside him.

"Do you think Mom sees us right now?" he suddenly asked.

I paused to ponder. "I don't know, David. I think maybe she does see us. Why do you ask?"

"I don't see how she could, Dad. I thought Heaven was full of happiness. How could she bear to see us so sad?"

Could Lynda witness our pain in Heaven? How could that be possible? How could she bear it? "I think she does see us," I finally said. "But she sees the whole story, including how it all turns out, which is beautiful to her. It's going to be a good story, David."

Sittser added: "I would not hazard to estimate the number of times I have been asked, "How does Christianity address the problem of suffering?" … The Christian answer to suffering [is] Christ's suffering [and] Christ's resurrection …. God knows pain within himself; God knows joy within himself. He knows the whole story as one, including how it all turns out, which is glorious indeed."

Reflection Question:

How does your heart react to the idea that life is going to be a good story in spite of suffering, because we have an Everlasting Father who loves us?

Week 3 Bible Study – Isaiah 64 – Everlasting Father

Open
- How did you see the truth of God's Good News of wanting us to know Him this week?
- When you were a teenager, did you ever get in trouble trying to rebel against your parents' authority? How did they respond?

Dig *(Read the passage: Isaiah 64)*

1. What questions, concerns, new things did you discover?
2. What does the tone of the prayer in v. 1-4 tell you about the emotional state of Isaiah the prophet? About his real desire?
3. Where in your life now do you wish God would do something? How does that affect your prayers?
4. When you pray, do you express to God the full range of your emotions? Which ones do you hid from Him?
5. What images does Isaiah use to describe God? How do these images show the father nature of God?
6. How does Isaiah describe the work the people tried to do to please God? (v. 6)
7. How does Isaiah describe our relationship to God in v. 8? What does it mean to be clay in a potter's hand?
8. How does it change your image of yourself to know you are the work of God's hand?

Apply
1. What did you learn about God? (His character, ways, concerns)
2. What did you learn about people? (yourself?)
3. What does God do for us? In what way does this point to what Jesus does for us that we can't do on our own? How is this passage Good News rather than Good Advice?
4. What do we (I) need to do?
5. Who do I need to share this with?

Pray - Thank you / Sorry / Please

8 Now, therefore, thus you shall say to my servant David, 'Thus says the Lord of hosts, I took you from the pasture, from following the sheep, that you should be prince over my people Israel. 9 And I have been with you wherever you went and have cut off all your enemies from before you. And I will make for you a great name, like the name of the great ones of the earth. 10 And I will appoint a place for my people Israel and will plant them, so that they may dwell in their own place and be disturbed no more. And violent men shall afflict them no more, as formerly, 11 from the time that I appointed judges over my people Israel. And I will give you rest from all your enemies. Moreover, the Lord declares to you that the Lord will make you a house.

12 When your days are fulfilled and you lie down with your fathers, I will raise up your offspring after you, who shall come from your body, and I will establish his kingdom. 13 He shall build a house for my name, and I will establish the throne of his kingdom forever. 14 I will be to him a father, and he shall be to me a son. When he commits iniquity, I will discipline him with the rod of men, with the stripes of the sons of men, 15 but my steadfast love will not depart from him, as I took it from Saul, whom I put away from before you. 16 And your house and your kingdom shall be made sure forever before me. Your throne shall be established forever.'" 17 In accordance with all these words, and in accordance with all this vision, Nathan spoke to David.

Devotional

The King Visits the Earth:

Jesus is the rightful King of all creation, the wonderful counselor, the mighty God, the everlasting father to his people -- and He deserves incredible honor. David, the first honorable sovereign of Israel sat on a borrowed seat. Knowing that reality, in 2 Samuel 7 David realizes the silliness of the situation. David notes that while he sleeps in royal beds and sits on royal thrones the Lord is, in essence, camping in a tent outside the gates. In David's mind it just doesn't seem right. The solution: Build God a house.

But that just doesn't make sense, either. God doesn't need a house -- nor does he really want one. Instead, God wants a people. So, in this incredible chapter, God promises to fulfill all the covenants made before through the line of David and rather than merely creating a house for David -- he promises to make David "a house". In other words, to create a dynasty that will culminate in the Prince of Peace coming to bring terms of peace to a people of no peace.

Athanasius, who wrote the incredible, "On the Incarnation" write this:

Some may ask, Why did [Jesus] not manifest himself by means of other and nobler parts of creation such as sun or moon or stars or fire or air, instead of mere man? The answer is this: the Lord did not come to make a display. He came to heal and to teach suffering people. For one who wanted to make a display, the thing would have been just to appear and dazzle the beholders. But for him who came to heal and to teach, the way was not merely to dwell here but to put himself at the disposal of those who needed him.

This "dynasty promised" will wind its way through history in many great kings and many not-so great -- but will culminate in one who will take a throne that "shall be established forever". That one is Jesus who comes to establish his reign on the throne of every human heart.

Reflection Question

When are there times in your life that you are tempted to put on a display in your spiritual life to dazzle others? What would it look like to be "established forever" in Jesus the true Prince of Peace?

Week 4   Day 2   Psalm 132: 8-19

8 Arise, O Lord, and go to your resting place, you and the ark of your might. 9 Let your priests be clothed with righteousness and let your saints shout for joy.
10 For the sake of your servant David, do not turn away the face of your anointed one.

11 The Lord swore to David a sure oath from which he will not turn back, "One of the sons of your body I will set on your throne. 12 If your sons keep my covenant and my testimonies that I shall teach them, their sons also forever shall sit on your throne."

13 For the Lord has chosen Zion; he has desired it for his dwelling place: 14 "This is my resting place forever; here I will dwell, for I have desired it. 15 I will abundantly bless her provisions; I will satisfy her poor with bread. 16 Her priests I will clothe with salvation, and her saints will shout for joy. 17 There I will make a horn to sprout for David; I have prepared a lamp for my anointed. 18 His enemies I will clothe with shame, but on him his crown will shine."

Devotional

In September 2013, Britain's Prince William, who is second in line to the throne after his father Prince Charles, completed a three-year stint as a Royal Air Force search-and-rescue helicopter pilot. In March of 2015 the 32-year-old prince took up his new job as an air ambulance pilot as an employee of Bond Air Services. Kensington Palace announced William's new job, based at Cambridge airport in eastern England, will involve responding to emergencies ranging from road traffic accidents to heart attacks. He will reportedly be paid an annual salary of USD $59,000, but will donate it in full to charity.

This story from the Business Standard Journal made world news headlines, but the story of the Bible is far more surprising. The King of Kings doesn't just commandeer a helicopter and rescue us from above. He descends into our mess, dies in that mess, and then rescues us not just from accidents but from our own sin.

At the end of David's life, God makes a promise to David that his descendants will be on the throne of Israel forever. This promise is deepened with the awareness that the True King Jesus will come from David's line.

Jesus doesn't come that first time as a military commander, a political king, or a pompous reigning monarch. He comes humble and lowly, with angels announcing him as the Prince of Peace.

When you think about it, military might or political savvy are not what we need to free our hearts. Peace is needed both in the world and in our hearts and lives. Jesus comes, bearing peace—both peace with God and man. He solidified that peace by reconciling us to God through his death on the cross and resurrection in the body. That is truly lasting peace!

Reflection Question

Where in your life or relationships do you need the Prince of Peace to give you peace this Advent season?

Week 4 Day 3 Romans 16:25-27

[25] *Now to him who is able to strengthen you according to my gospel and the preaching of Jesus Christ, according to the revelation of the mystery that was kept secret for long ages* [26] *but has now been disclosed and through the prophetic writings has been made known to all nations, according to the command of the eternal God, to bring about the obedience of faith—* [27] *to the only wise God be glory forevermore through Jesus Christ! Amen.*

Devotional

The Prophets had foretold of a mighty God who would come and take the throne. Might and majesty deployed for the sake of justice. The King who was coming would oppose and defeat every form of pervasive unrighteousness. The picture in our mind most certainly is of power being thrown down.

And yet, when Jesus comes -- well, he's not that impressive. He has the opportunity (twice!) to raise an army of thousands as he feeds them on the hillside. He has the ability to unite warring political factions -- if he's just take a clear swipe at Rome. He has the following of intellectuals who quietly admire and the people who are openly amazed.

Yet, in every instance, Jesus walks away from political power and right into the arms of powerlessness. Or so it seems.

Peter Larson, reflecting on this Prince of Peace, notes the amazing irony. When Jesus says "no" to the cult of power that could so easily be obtained through politics, popularity or personal power -- one would assume that he's just not the mighty, wonderful, everlasting power that they'd been waiting for. But Jesus has a different way of becoming the Prince of Peace:

Despite our efforts to keep him out, God intrudes. The life of Jesus is bracketed by two impossibilities: a virgin's womb and an empty tomb. Jesus entered our world through a door marked "No Entrance" and left through a door marked "No Exit."

Reflection Question

How do you need Jesus' peace to strengthen you this Advent? Where is your "No Exit" and "No Entrance" that the Prince of Peace can calm?

Week 4 Day 4 Colossians 1:15-20

¹⁵ *He is the image of the invisible God, the firstborn of all
creation.* ¹⁶ *For by him all things were created, in heaven and on
earth, visible and invisible, whether thrones or dominions or rulers
or authorities—all things were created through him and for him.*

¹⁷ *And he is before all things, and in him all things hold
together.* ¹⁸ *And he is the head of the body, the church. He is the
beginning, the firstborn from the dead, that in everything he might
be preeminent.* ¹⁹ *For in him all the fullness of God was pleased to
dwell,* ²⁰ *and through him to reconcile to himself all things, whether
on earth or in heaven, making peace by the blood of his cross.*

Devotional

Most kingdoms do anything they can to protect their king. This is
the unspoken premise of the game of chess, for example. When
the king falls, the kingdom is lost. Therefore, the king must be
protected at all costs.

Another notable example comes from the Allied invasion of
Normandy on D-Day, June 6, 1944. British Prime Minister Winston
Churchill desperately wanted to join the expeditionary forces and
watch the invasion from the bridge of a battleship in the English
Channel. U.S. General Dwight David Eisenhower was desperate
to stop him, for fear that the Prime Minister might be killed in
battle. When it became apparent that Churchill would not be
dissuaded, Eisenhower appealed to a higher authority: King
George VI. The king went and told Churchill that if it was the Prime
Minister's duty to witness the invasion, he could only conclude that
it was also his own duty as king to join him on the battleship. At
this point Churchill reluctantly agreed to back down, for he knew
that he could never expose the King of England to such danger.

Philip Ryken, in his sermon "Long Live the King!", says:

> *King Jesus did exactly the opposite. With royal courage
> he surrendered his body to be crucified. On the cross*

he offered a king's ransom: his life for the life of his people. He would die for all the wrong things that we had ever done and would do, completely atoning for all our sins. The crown of thorns that was meant to make a mockery of his royal claims actually proclaimed his kingly dignity, even in death.

We see in the Colossians passage the absolute power and authority that Jesus holds. Look at what Paul states about Him— image of invisible God, firstborn of creation, before all things, head of the body—the church. These are amazing attributes of the authority of Jesus as King. We could spend years just studying those qualities. Yet, how does the passage conclude? It says that he gave those things up to reconcile us to God. This peace with God only came through Jesus's sacrifice for our sake on the cross. This is a King like no other—offering a peace like no other found on heaven and earth.

Reflection Question

How do the strong attributes of Jesus' Kingly power give depth to your understanding of the peace he offers? How do they signify that He is the only one who can bring this true peace as our Prince of Peace?

Week 4 Day 5 Luke 1:26-38

26 In the sixth month the angel Gabriel was sent from God to a city of Galilee named Nazareth, 27 to a virgin betrothed to a man whose name was Joseph, of the house of David. And the virgin's name was Mary. 28 And he came to her and said, "Greetings, O favored one, the Lord is with you!" 29 But she was greatly troubled at the saying, and tried to discern what sort of greeting this might be. 30 And the angel said to her, "Do not be afraid, Mary, for you have found favor with God. 31 And behold, you will conceive in your womb and bear a son, and you shall call his name Jesus. 32 He will be great and will be called the Son of the Most High. And the Lord God will give to him the throne of his father David, 33 and he will reign over the house of Jacob forever, and of his kingdom there will be no end."

34 And Mary said to the angel, "How will this be, since I am a virgin?"

35 And the angel answered her, "The Holy Spirit will come upon you, and the power of the Most High will overshadow you; therefore the child to be born will be called holy—the Son of God. 36 And behold, your relative Elizabeth in her old age has also conceived a son, and this is the sixth month with her who was called barren. 37 For nothing will be impossible with God." 38 And Mary said, "Behold, I am the servant of the Lord; let it be to me according to your word." And the angel departed from her.

Devotional

In the 1960s Mary Ellen Rothrock was a grad student in English literature at the University of Wisconsin. In 1998 she wrote in Christian Reader magazine:

Despair seemed to permeate the student body, especially those in the humanities. A fellow graduate student summed it up cynically, "Playwright Samuel Becket is right. Man is just a piece of trash in a universe that's running down."

In college, atheism became my religion. Yet when I got into grad school, I found myself seeking to fill a spiritual void in my life. I began practicing Transcendental Meditation (TM). I met periodically with a TM supervisor. After a year or so of meditating, I mentioned that I had a recurring thought when I was trying to concentrate on my mantra. 'It's a line from Handel's Messiah. Something in my mind keeps repeating "And the glory of the Lord shall be revealed."

To my young mind, not only was the music thrilling, but the words seemed to come from beyond this world. I loved the joyful language: 'Hallelujah! for the Lord God Omnipotent reigneth. ... For unto us a Child is born … And the glory of the Lord shall be revealed, and all flesh shall see it together.;"

Her TM supervisor told her to ignore the words that kept coming to her but "I told myself, 'These aren't just random thoughts.' It suddenly hit me. The phrase "And the glory of the Lord" shall be revealed was an invitation from a personal God of glory to seek him! Why couldn't he be 'Wonderful, Counselor, the mighty God, the everlasting Father, the Prince of Peace?'

Within months, she met a woman who explained how she could have a personal relationship with Jesus Christ. She said, "As I heard the words from the Bible, the words from the musical score made sense. The Holy Spirit convinced me of the truth: the God I'd hungered for, the personal God, loved me. 'Hallelujah! For the Lord God Omnipotent reigneth.'"

Reflection Question

What does it mean for the glory of the Lord to be revealed in your life? How can His glory bring you peace as He comes as the Prince of Peace?

Week 4   Bible Study- 2 Samuel 7:4-17 Prince of Peace

Open

1. How did you see the truth of God's Word at work in your life
    this past week? Were you able to encourage anyone or share
    the Good News with them?
2. Describe the house you lived in as a 10-year-old. How did it
    compare to your neighbors?

Dig (*Read the passage: 2 Samuel 7:4-17*)

1. What questions, concerns, new things did you discover?
2. Where did God dwell with the Israelites during their time in the
    desert?
3. Why does God remind David of his past dwelling place?
4. Why does God say "no" to David building him a temple? Who
    does God say will build His temple?
5. What promises does God make to David? How do you think
    David felt about these promises?
6. Who is the one prophesied to be on David's throne forever?
    (v. 13)
7. Do you tend to favor God by working for him? Or savor God
    by worshipping him? Why is that?

Apply
1. What did you learn about God? (His character, ways, concerns)
2. What did you learn about people? (yourself?)
3. What does God do for us? In what way does this point to what
Jesus does for us that we can't do on our own? How is this
passage Good News rather than Good Advice?
4. What do we (I) need to do?
5. Who do I need to share this with?

Pray - Thank you / Sorry / Please

<u>Two Ways to Live Notes</u>

Please purchase and use You, Me and the Bible from MatthiasMedia.com with those you are discipling. Information below.

Genesis 1:26-31
Revelation 4:6-11
How is the Creator and creation described here? What happened??

Genesis 3:1-6
Romans 1:18-25
What will God do about rebellion?

Deuteronomy 29:16-20
Hebrews 9:27
Romans 6:23
Is that it then? Just death and ruin?

Isaiah 53:3-10
Romans 5:8
1 Peter 2:22-24, 3:18
Why did Jesus die?

Acts 2:22-24, 36
Acts 17:22-32
What fresh start does the Resurrection of Jesus offer?

John 3:16-18, 36
What is the result of our way? God's way?
Which way do I want to live?

<u>**Discipleship Engines (RLM)**</u>

- ***Definition of a Disciple (Mark 1:17)***
  - "Come, follow me": a disciple knows and follows Christ (head).
  - "And I will make you": a disciple is being changed by Christ (heart).
  - "Fishers of men": a disciple is committed to the mission of Christ (hands).
- ***Method of Discipleship***
  - Jesus was an intentional leader
  - Jesus did His disciple-making in a relational environment
  - Jesus followed a process that can be learned and repeated.
  - An intentional leader + a relational environment + a reproducible process = an infinite number of disciples.
- ***Five Stages of a Disciple's Growth***
  - Spiritually dead (unbelief)
  - Spiritual infant (ignorance)
  - Spiritual child (self-centeredness)
  - Spiritual young adult (service, God-centeredness, other-centeredness)
  - Spiritual parent (intentionality, reproducibility, strategy)
- ***Moving Disciples Forward***
  - Spiritually Dead: share the gospel
  - Spiritual infant: share your life, share new truth, share new habits
  - Spiritual child: connect to God, connect to small group, connect to God's purpose
  - Spiritual young adult: equip for ministry, provide ministry opportunities, release to do ministry
  - Spiritual parent: explain discipleship process, release to disciple another with your help, release to disciple alone
- ***Mastering the Discipleship Process (SCMD)***
  - Moving the spiritually dead toward life: Share
  - Nurturing spiritual infants: Share
  - Guiding spiritual children: Connect
  - Training spiritual young adults: Minister
  - Releasing spiritual parents: Disciple
- ***Main Engine: Small Group Bible-storying method (called Orality)***
  - What new thing did you discover in the story?
  - What did you learn about God?
  - What did you learn about people?
  - Which person is most like you in the story?
  - What will you take away from this discussion?
  - What will you do with what you have learned?

Principles for Studying a Bible Passage

#1 Stay on the Line - We *must stay on the line of Scripture, never straying above it or below it*

Diagnostic Questions
- What does the text say?
- Where is that found in the text?

Strategies: Be aware of both extremes, anticipate how those who farthest above and the farthest below might treat the text, test consistency of your reading with the rest of Scripture

#2 Let the Text shape your Framework - *We must let the Bible shape our frameworks rather than letting our frameworks shape our interpretations of the Bible*

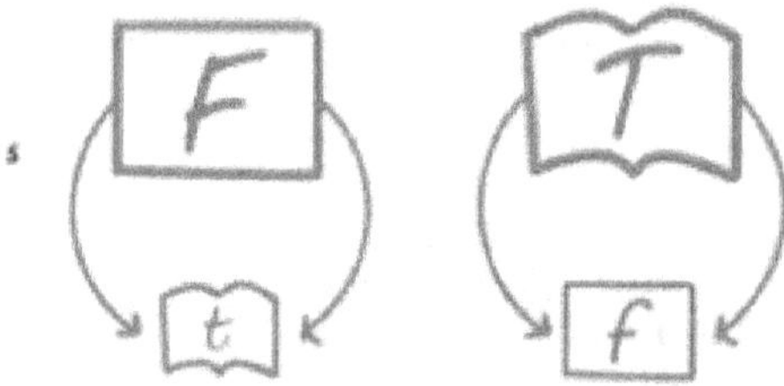

Diagnostic Questions
- What pre-conceptions am I bringing to the text?
- How would the original hearers understand this?

Strategies: Identify your own frameworks (ideological, political, theological, etc.), constantly approach the text with fresh eyes, consult many different translations of the Bible (e.g. dynamic, literal, paraphrase

#3 Look for Context - *We must understand the context in order to see how the original audience understood the text*

<u>Diagnostic Question</u>: Why has the author put this passage here (at this place) in the book?

<u>Strategies</u>: Read the chapter on both sides of your text, read the entire book, if paired with another book, then read both books (e.g., 1 and 2 Corinthians), know where your passage is specifically in historical context and read any corresponding passages (e.g., read 1 or 2 Samuel for some Psalms, read Acts for some Pauline epistles)

#4 Travel Through the Cross - *If we are to teach the Bible as Christians, we must show a legitimate connection from our text to the gospel of Jesus Christ.*

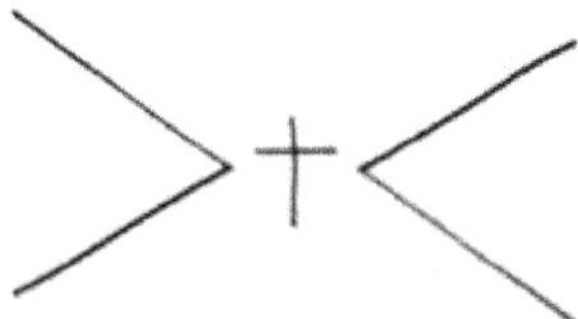

<u>Strategies</u>: note any cross-references to the other Testament, develop a good sense of Biblical Theology, consider historical fulfillment and theological themes, use typology and analogy (including contrast and irony), know how key doctrines relate

<u>Diagnostic Question</u>: How does my passage relate to the gospel (narrowly defined as the death and resurrection of Jesus Christ)?

<u>**Acknowledgements**</u>

Scripture quotations are from the ESV® Bible (The Holy Bible, English Standard Version®), copyright © 2001 by Crossway, a publishing ministry of Good News Publishers. Used by permission. All rights reserved.

This book rests upon the work of many commentaries, seminary notes and classes. If you've been quoted without attribution, please contact us so that we can make it right.

Authors and Editors

Anna Goodwin Smith
Everett Goodwin
Gregory M. Smith

Iona Network exists to welcome people home with Good News and help them their next step as they follow their leader, are formed in love, and fulfill their great purpose

The Rev. Gregory M. Smith has led this effort through church planting, mission outreach, and seminary classes.

www.ingramcontent.com/pod-product-compliance
Lightning Source LLC
Chambersburg PA
CBHW071511130726
47997CB00006B/2496